I DRIVE A VALENCE

THE COLLECTED LYRICS OF BILL CALLAHAN

Drag City Incorporated | Chicago

Drag City Web Address: www.dragcity.com

Printed in the United States of America
Library of Congress Control Number: 2014945705
ISBN: 978-1-937112-15-8

Cover design: Jaime Zuverza

Second Edition

For Kaua'i

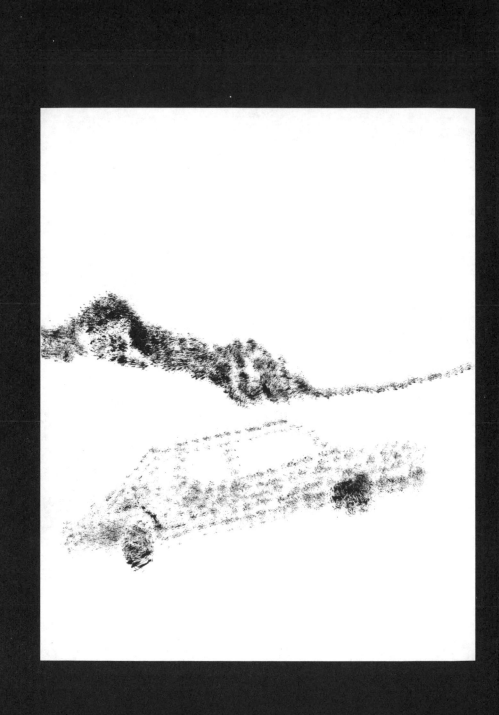

Lyrics

Illustrations

What's next?

All Thoughts are Prey to Some Beast

The leafless tree looked like a brain
The birds within were all the thoughts and desires within me
Hopping around from branch to branch
Or snug in their nests listening in

An eagle came over the horizon
And shook the branches with its sight
The softer thoughts: starlings finches and wrens
The softer thoughts they all took flight

The eagle looked clear through the brain tree
Empty he thought save for me
Maybe I'll make this one my home
Consolidate the nests of the tiny
Raise a family of might like me

Then something struck him wings of bone
Sweet desires and soft thoughts were all gone
The eagle shrieked
I'm alone!

Well it was time to flee the tree
The eagle snuck up on the wind
One talon at a time
Being Sky King of the sky
What did he have to fear?

All thoughts are prey to some beast
All thoughts are prey to some beast

Sweet desire and soft thoughts return to me
Sweet desire and soft thoughts return to me
Sweet desire and soft thoughts return to me

A Man Needs A Woman or A Man to Be A Man

When you leave I go into our room
And lay me down on birds of paradise

It's pretty womanly in here!
Roses noting every move
Nothing goes on except what should
A vast legacy of good
And I don't know if I can uphold it on my own
I don't know if I can uphold it on my own
I don't know if I'm to be trusted
In our room
Alone

A man needs a woman or a man to be a man

The light is explicit between nine and noon
The light shows a life to things thought dead
Like oaken legs and fireworks beneath the bed

Fireworks are wasted in the day
I set 'em off anyway
To pass the time 'til you return
I can't see a thing 'til you return
Maybe a little smoke 'til you return
With fireworks
More fireworks!
And you tell me to wait
Just wait

A man needs a woman or a man to be a man

And when it's good and dark
The sky a wet black
Like earth has turned
You say OK
Now is time OK
Like earth has turned

Above us explode a golden lion dripping red
A blue bear spitting white
A spider of fire on a web of sparks
A green dragon with spiraled eyes
Fireworks light the way!
Fireworks light the way!

Before us lie many a night
Before us lie fireworks in boxes
But only in you deep in you
Is the fire that lights them

A man needs a woman or a man to be a man

America!

America!
America!
America!
America!
You are so grand and golden
Oh I wish I was deep in America tonight

America!
America!
I watch David Letterman in Australia
Oh America!
You are so grand and golden
I wish I was on the next flight
To America!

Captain Kristofferson!
Buck Sergeant Newbury!
Leatherneck Jones!
Sergeant Cash!
What an Army!
What an Air Force!
What a Marines!
America!
(I never served my country)
America!
America!

Afghanistan!
Vietnam!
Iran!
Native Americon!
America!
Everyone's allowed a past
They don't care to mention
America!
America!

Well it's hard to rouse a hog in delta
And it can get tense around the Bible belt
America!
America!

The lucky suckle teat
Others chaw pig-knuckle meat
Ain't enough teat ain't enough teat
Ain't enough to eat
In America
America! America!

Baby's Breath

There grows a weed looks like a flower
Looks like baby's breath on a mirror

My girl and I rushed atop the altar
The sacrifice was made
It was not easy undertaking
The root's grip sucked like a living grave

Oh young girl at the wedding
Baby's breath in her hair
A crowning lace above her face
That will last a day
Before it turns to hay

Good plans are made by hand
I'd cut a clearing in the land
For a little bed for her to cry comfortable in

Each day I looked out on the lawn
And I wondered what all was gone
Until I saw it was lucky old me
How could I run without losing anything?
How could I run without becoming lean?
It was agreed it was a greed
It was me tearing out the baby's breath

Oh I am a helpless man
So help me
I'm on my knees
Gardening
It was not a weed it was a flower
My baby's gone oh where has my baby gone?
She was not a weed she was a flower

And now I know you must reap what you sow
Or sing
Yes now I know you must reap what you sow
Or sing!

Bathysphere

When I was seven
I asked my mother
To trip me to the bay
And put me on a ship

Lower me down
Lower me out of here
Because when I was seven
I wanted to live in a bathysphere

Blue green coral
A silent eel
I can really feel a dream down here

And if the water should cut my line
Set me free
If the water should cut my line
Set me free
I'll be the lost sailor
My home is the sea

But when I was seven
My father said to me
You can't swim

And I never dreamed of the sea again

Blood Red Bird

I was not woken by the rooster
Nor by the crow's tough song
But the midnight cry of a blood red bird
Brought this sleeplessness on

Threw open the window
Moonlight on a black garden of thorns
And the cool wind on my sweat

What cries home
Where cries from
A blood red bird lies in the woods
Weeping into dead leaves
With wing torn and jutting bone

What hand bent it to bust
To be useless
What hand I could have done it
With two fingers

A blood red bird
A blood red bird

We can continually sink into each other
Just deep enough to rip out a bit more flesh
When we move away
A scarf of skin trailing out behind

Like an arrow
I was only passing through
A blood red bird
A blood red bird

Bowery

My grandfather died a Bowery bum
My grandfather died the son of an Irish man
On the Bowery

Oh the Bowery!

My father tried
To find his bones
And to his trials
I added my own

Oh the Bowery!

Well I'm new here
Where can a fella eat?
I'm new here
Where can a fella sleep?
I'm new here
And I've got a pit in my gut
On the Bowery
Way down on the Bowery

Oh the Bowery!

My grandfather left my father twice
Second time was on his wife's advice
Straight back to the Bowery

Oh the Bowery!

And when he came up from the river of Methadone
He took his last breath on the Bowery

Oh the Bowery!

Cold Blooded Old Times

Cold blooded old times
The type of memories
That turn your bones to glass

Mother came rushing in
She said we didn't see a thing
We said we didn't see a thing

And father left at eight
Nearly splintering the gate
Cold blooded old times

The type of memories
That turn your bones to glass

And though you were
Just a little squirrel
You understood every word

And in this way
They gave you clarity
A cold blooded clarity

Cold blooded old times

How can I stand
And laugh with the man
Who redefined your body?

In those cold blooded old times

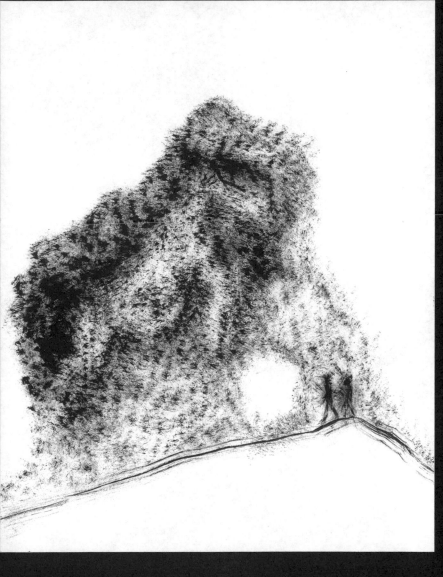

Day

Some people are a sickness on this land
They're killing they're taking they're stealing whatever they can
Anything anything anything that is not bolted down
Your life your money your heart your faith your bike
Anything anything anything that is not bolted down

Learn from the animals
Monkeys do
Monkeys do piggish things too
Learn from the vegetables
Monkeys do
The way they strive toward the light
A small potato in the blight still strives toward the light
I know it's as dark as night
It's as dark as night

It is day though

Some would ask what are we to do
With a world that crumbles to the touch?
A world that spins and dies where it stands
Like trying ain't enough?

To family is all you can do
Even if it's just us two
To family is all you can do

And strive toward the light
It's as dark as night
Strive towards the light
I know it's as dark as night

It is day though

Dress Sexy at My Funeral

Dress sexy at my funeral my good wife
For the first time in your life

Wear your blouse undone to here
And your skirt split up to there

Dress sexy at my funeral my good wife
For the first time in your life

Wink at the minister
Blow kisses to my grieving brothers

Dress sexy at my funeral my good wife

And when it comes your turn to speak
Before the crowd
Tell them about the time we did it
On the beach with fireworks above us
On the railroad tracks
With the gravel in your back
In the back room of a crowded bar
And in the very graveyard
Where my body now rests

Dress sexy at my funeral my good wife
For the first time in your life

Also tell them about how I gave to charity
And tried to love my fellow man
As best I could
But most of all don't forget about the time
On the beach
With fireworks above us

Drinking at the Dam

I remember drinking at the dam
With the jarheads on the other side
Warm beer and tearing up the cans
And all of us yelling abuse
Cutting school to go drinking at the dam

Skin mags in the brambles
For the first part of my life
I thought women had orange skin
It was the first part of my life
Second is the rest

And now teenage warchests fill
And do the dirty dirty work
It was the first part of their lives

Drinking at the dam
Holding back what I can
But the power is so much

Drinking at the dam
Holding back what I can
I'm just drinking at the dam

Drover

The real people went away
I'll find a better word
Someday
Leaving only me and my dreams
My cattle
And a resonator

I drove all the beasts down
Right under your nose
The lumbering footloose power
The bull and the rose
Don't touch them don't try to hurt them
My cattle!

I drove them by the crops
And thought the crops were lost
I consoled myself with rudimentary thoughts
And I set my watch
Against the city clock
It was way off

One thing about this wild wild country
It takes a strong strong
It breaks a strong strong mind
Yeah one thing about this wild wild country
It takes a strong strong
It breaks a strong strong mind

And anything less anything less
Makes me feel like I'm wasting my time
But the pain and frustration is not mine
It belongs to the cattle
Through the valley

And when my cattle turns on me
I was knocked back flat
Knocked out cold
For one clack of the train track
Then I rose a colossal hand buried
Buried in sand
I rose like a drover
For I am in the end a drover
A drover by trade!

And when my cattle turns on me
I am a drover double fold

My cattle bears it all away for me and everyone

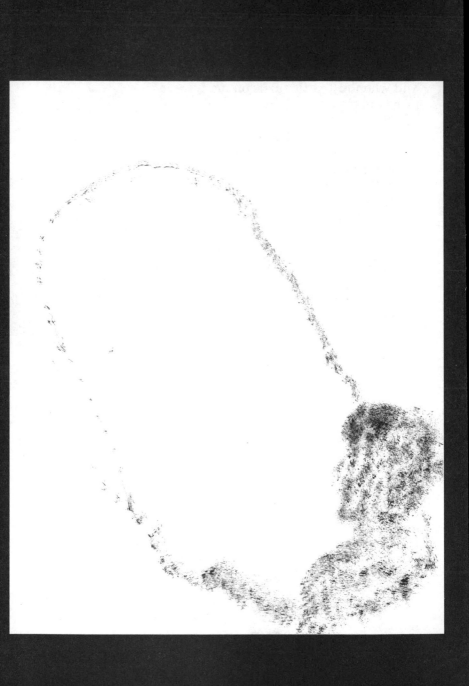

Eid Ma Clack Shaw

(Working through dads' pain...)

Last night I swear I felt your touch
Gentle and warm
The hair stood on my arms
How how how?
Show me the way show me the way
Show me the way to shake a memory
I flipped my forelock I twitched my withers
I reared and bucked
I could not put my rider aground
All these fine memories are fucking me down
I dreamed it was a dream that you were gone
I woke up feeling so ripped by reality

Love is the king of the beasts
And when it gets hungry it must kill to eat
Love is the king of the beasts
A lion walking down city streets

I fell back asleep some time later on
And I dreamed the perfect song
It held all the answers like hands laid on
I woke halfway and scribbled it down
And in the morning what I wrote I read
It was hard to read at first but here's what it said:

Eid ma clack shaw zuboven del bah
Murteppy vin seener cofally rackdah

Show me the way show me the way
Show me the way to shake a memory

Eid ma clack shaw zuboven del bah
Murteppy vin seener cofally rackdah

Show me the way show me the way
Show me the way
To shake a memory

Ex-Con

Whenever I get dressed up
I feel like an ex-con
Trying to make good

Jean jacket and tie
Feel like such a lie
When I go to your house
I feel like I'm
Casing the joint
In the grocery store
In line behind a mother and child
I'm gonna take that child
I'm gonna take that child

See 'cause alone in my room
I feel like such a part of the community
But out on the streets
I feel like a robot by the river

Alone in my room
I feel such a warmth for the community
But out on the streets
Out on the streets
I feel like a robot by the river
Looking for a drink

Faith/Void

It's time to put God away

Damning the children
Making the ill just a little more sick

It's time to put God away
(I put God away)

This is the end of faith
No more must I strive
To find my peace
To find my peace in a lie

It's time to put God away
(I put God away)

For a void without a question is just perverse
Like tear gas misters at my grave

It's time to put God away
(I put God away)

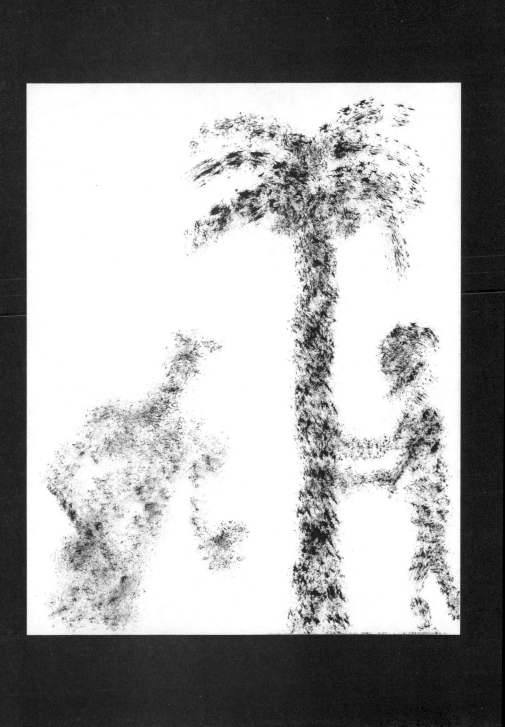

Finer Days

Granted passage
Into the finer days
How I got here I do not know
And if it were all to disappear
I would not know how to return

And all of my old friends
They want me to stay down down down with them
I could extend them a hand
But they would only pull it off
In their grasp
In their powder

And so I find myself isolated
Isolated in these fine fine days

Fools' Lament

I been good
Poifect
I'm already ready
For my great reward

Mountain and river
Stopping to swim
You can't everyday
Could we?

I must reach the clearing
My vision is failing
I see things clearly
Or not at all
It is that fools' lament

I've taken the edge off
So many times
I'm round

The sculptor too long
Ends in dust
An admirer of women
He tried to make a bust
He didn't know when to stop
Chipping
Chippin
Chip-p
Chip
Chip
Chi

Humiliation is good
It means you believe in something
My comeuppance I embrace
Like a monkey dressed just like me
It is that fools' lament
It is that fools' lament

Be a man
Be a man
Be a man
Be a woman

I wonder what kind of human that is?

Free's

I'm standing in a field
A field of questions
As far as the eye can see
Is this what it means to be free?
Or is this what it means to belong to the free?

To be free in bad times and good
To belong to being derided for things I don't believe
And lauded for things I did not do

If this is what it means to be free
Then I'm free and I belong to the free
And the free
They belong to me

Garb

God
God
God
Garb

Hangman Blues

Life's a joke
A waiting game now.
A juggling of vices
Tiny tiny vices
And they don't anchor me
To the ground
I know who the hangman is
So life's a joke

Ha ha ha
Ha ha ha

The clocks on the wall
Creeps higher
Save save
Restraint restraint
It's a joke
And I know who the hangman is

A ship in a vial
A headstone on the wharf
And it will pin me
To the ground

Ha ha ha
Ha ha ha

All the lights look green
So unbend your toughest smile
I think we've got

One more mile

The Hard Road

I'll take the hard road
I believe I'll see you there
In a cyclone of stones
Wooden spikes in your hair
Or maybe you'll be resting
Leaning up against a busted fence
Pick a burr from your coat
And then we're back up on the hard road

We could sleep in a barn
Bathe in a lake
Steal a pie
Let hunger dictate
The steps we take
Along the hard road

And when Winter comes
We'll borrow from
The nearest washing line

And when Summer comes
It's almost impossible
Not to have a good time

Out on the hard road

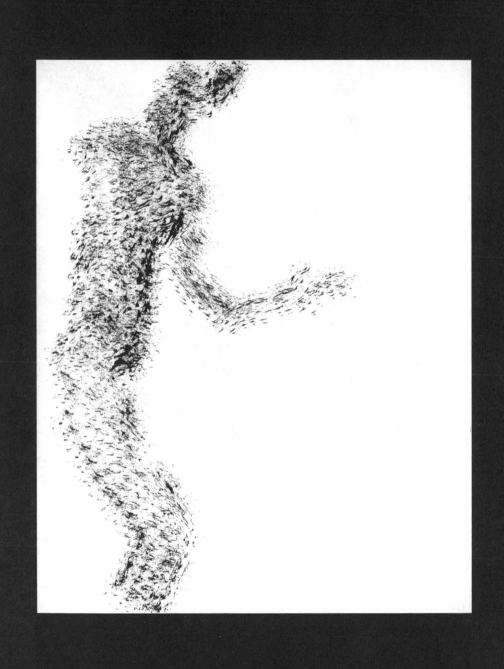

Held

For the first time in my life
I let myself be held
Like a big old baby
I surrendered
To your charity

I lay back in the tall tall grass
And let the ants cover me
I let the jets fly
Not wishing for their destruction
Orange and black in a perfect blue sky

For the first time in my life
I am moving away moving away moving away
From within the reach of me
And all the while I'm being held
Like a big old baby

Hit the Ground Running

I had to leave the country
Though there was some nice folk there
Now I don't know where I'm going
All I know is I'll hit the ground running

Boney cowboys
And Southern gentlemen
Betting women
That will never mend
They ride the roads as they bend
As they bend to their dead ends

I had to leave the country
Though there was some nice folk there
And now I don't know where I'm going
All I know is I'll hit the ground running

I was raised in a pit of snakes
Blink your eyes I was raised on cake
I couldn't memorize a century of slang
Or learn to tell the same story again and again and again oh!

I had to leave the country
Though there was some nice folk there
Now I don't know where I'm going
All I know is I'll hit the ground running

Bitterness is the lowest sin
A bitter man rots from within
I've seen his smile
Yellow and brown
The bitterness has brought him down

I had to leave the country
Though there was some nice folk there
Now I don't know where I'm going
All I know to do is hit the ground running

Honeymoon Child

You are a true honeymoon child
Conceived on an island in the sun
Heels dug in the white sand
Loved and adored from day one

Raised in the wild space between two hearts
Where vines climb trees toward the light
Running naked dragging a kite
Or your dress on a string

You bring out the soft side in everyone
We gather like ravens on a rusty scythe
Just to watch
Such a little dove
Just to watch such a little dove
Fly away

Mr. Bones from town said he saw you the other day
Said you'd changed but he wouldn't say how

It can always turn
It can always turn
A wing can always turn

I Break Horses

Well I rode out to the ocean
And the water looked like tarnished gold
I rode out on a broken horse who told me
She'd never felt so old

She asked me if I'd feed her
And ride her now and then
No no no
No no no
I break horses
I don't tend to them

I break horses
They seem to come to me
Asking to be broken
They seem to run to me

I break horses
It doesn't take me long
Just a few well placed words
And their wandering hearts are gone

At first her warmth felt good between my legs
A living breathing
Heart beating flesh
But soon that warmth turned to an itch
Turned to a scratch turned to a gash
I break horses
I don't tend to them

Tonight I'm swimming to my favorite island
And I don't want to see you swimming behind

I break horses
I don't tend to them

I Could Drive Forever

Too many lines have been broken
Too many people have crumbled apart in my hands

I should have left a long time ago
The best idea I ever had

With every mile another piece of me peels off
Whips down the road
All down the road

I feel light and strong
I could drive forever

I could drive forever

I Feel Like the Mother of the World

Whether or not there is any type of god
I'm not supposed to say
And today
I don't really care
God is a word
And the argument ends there
Oh do I feel like the mother of the world
With two children
Oh do I feel like the mother of the world
With two children fighting
When I was a boy I used to get into it bad
With my sister
And when the time came to face the truth
There'd be only tears and sides
Tears and sides
And my mother my poor mother
Would say it does not matter
It does not matter
Just stop fighting
Oh do I feel like the mother of the world
With two children

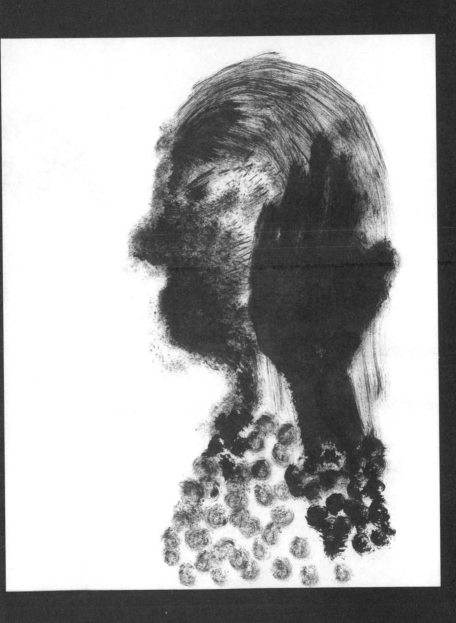

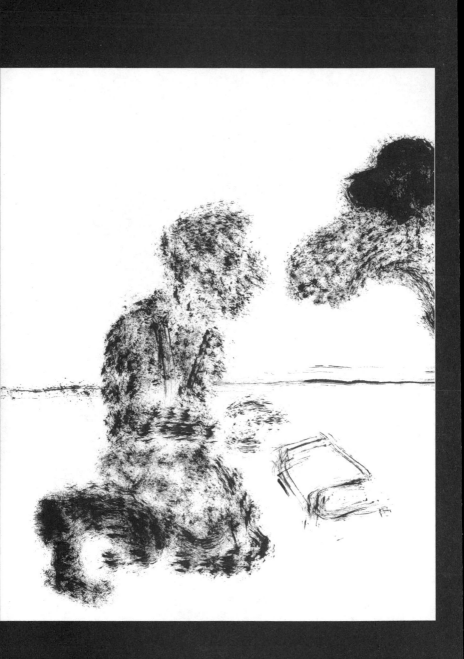

I'm New Here

I did not become someone different
I did not want to be
But I'm new here
Will you show me around?

No matter how far wrong you've gone
You can always turn around

Met a woman in a bar
Told her I was hard to get to know
And near impossible to forget
She said I had an ego on me
The size of Texas

Well I'm new here and I forget
Does that mean big or small?

And I'm shedding plates like a snake
And it may be crazy but I'm the closest thing I have
To a voice of reason

Turnaround turnaround turnaround
And you may come full circle and be new here again

Inspirational

If you're living the unliveable
By loving the unloveable
It's time to start changing the unchangeable
Be leaving the unleaveable

Come on

If you're living the unliveable
By loving the unloveable
It's time to start breaking
The unbreakable
And replacing the irreplaceable

Javelin Unlanding

You looked like worldwide Armageddon
While you slept
You looked so peaceful
It scared me

Don't die just yet
And leave me
Alone alone alone
On this journey
Round the sun

Oh! Javelin!
Oh! Javelin!
Unlanding!

Sometimes it's hard to know when
To call it an evening
See as much as we can stand
Stand til we stagger
Laying all twisted together and exposed
Like roots on a river bank

Bam bam bam!
The earth off its axis
The first draft's in ashes
And smeared on our faces

And oh! Javelin!

Jim Cain

I started out in search of ordinary things
How much of a tree bends in the wind
I started telling the story without knowing the end

I used to be darker
Then I got lighter
Then I got dark again
Something too big to be seen
Was passing over and over me

Well it seemed like a routine case at first
With the death of the shadow came a lightness of verse
But the darkest of nights in truth still dazzled
And I work myself until I'm frazzled

I ended up in search of ordinary things
Like how can a wave possibly be?
I started running when the concrete turned to sand
I started running when things didn't pan out as planned

If things go poorly and I not return
Remember the good things I done
In case things go poorly and I not return
Remember the good things I done

Or done me in

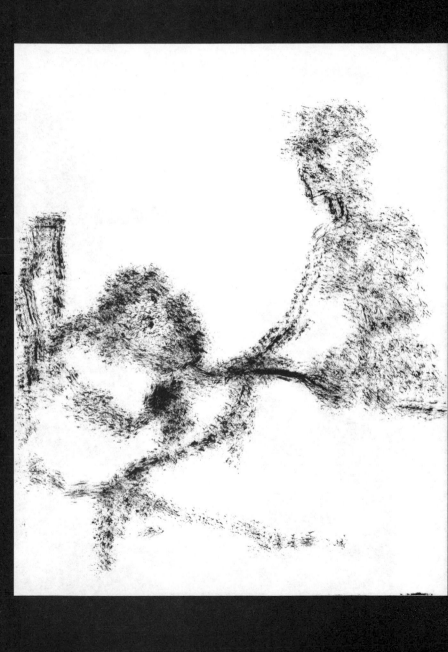

Justice Aversion

It happens on a side street maybe
It happens on a main street maybe
Lion bites zebra neck
Zebra stomps lion head

It's just this justice
Aversion
For the improper way
Things are done today

I route for the underdog
No matter who they are
Like the bank robber
In the getaway car

It's just this justice
Aversion
For the improper way
Things are done today

We could stay up all night talking
About my animal nature
And the universe's hesitance
To grant us grace

It could happen on a side street maybe
It could happen on a main street maybe

Keep Some Steady Friends Around

Keep some steady friends around
Best thing you can do
Keep some steady friends around
Best thing for you
Find a little place to go
When you have to get away
Find a little place to go
When you have to get away

But don't stay away too long
Because we love you too much
Don't stay away so long
Because we love you so much

To build your own house
Might be the best
Following your own design
Like some kind of god
With a fence all around
A fence all around

But don't forget to put in a gate
Don't forget to put in a gate
So you can have some steady friends come around
You can have some steady friends come around

Someone asked me just the other day
About souls and such
And if I believed in Judgement Day

Let Me See the Colts

Knocked on your door at dawn
With a spark in my heart
Dragged you from your bed
And said let me see the colts

Let me see the colts
That will run next year
Show them to a gambling man
Thinking of the future

Have you been drinking?
No nor sleeping
The all-knowing all-seeing eye is dog tired
And just wants to see the colts

We walked out through
The dew dappled brambles
And sat upon the fence

Is there anything as still as sleeping horses?
Is there anything as still as sleeping horses?

Garcia Reed shade off

Let's Move to the Country

Let's move to the country
Just you and me

My travels are over
My travels are through

Let's move to the country
Just me and you

A goat and a monkey
A mule and a flea

Let's move to the country
Just you and me

Let's start a...
Let's have a...

My travels are over

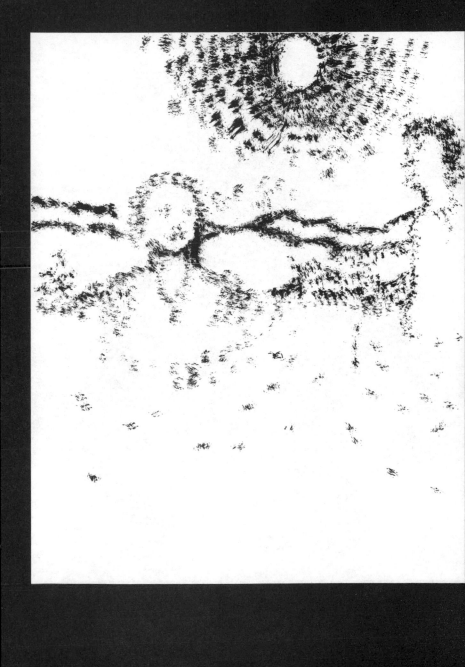

Live As if Someone is Always Watching You

Live as if someone is always watching you
In all you do
Live as if someone is always watching you

Eventually you will find
That both of you will need to come to some
Compromise
Maybe one or the other could agree
To sleep at different times
Or go off alone
Or at least shut their eye

Shut your eye off once in a while
Shut your eye off once in a while

So at least one of us
Can with some conviction say:

I am not of this glutty room
Or of this flubby body

My Friend

I looked all around
It was not written down
And so I'll tell you now
I will always love you
My friend

Now I'm not saying we're cut from the same tree
But like two pieces of the gallows
The pillar and the beam
Like two pieces of the gallows
We share a common dream—
To destroy what will harm other men
My friend

I looked all around
It was not written down
So I'll tell you now
I will always love you
My friend

Morality

I could kiss you
The sunlight coming in through your blouse
Words won't tell me what your body's all about

I could take you
You could take me
With hands and hair and eyes and bones and
knees

But hey
What would my wife say
What would my wife say
If I was married

I could keep you
With money every month
Some city apartment where I
Where you will stay

But hey
What would my wife say
What would my wife say
If I was married

Night

We do not know
How things work
We do not know
Where you go
In the night
Through the door
Through the door that holds you
Through the door that holds you
Out of the blue

We do not know
The door that holds you
Silent as glue
We stand under it
But we don't understand it
The door that holds you
Silent as glue

And stars fall on
Stars fall on
Silent as glue

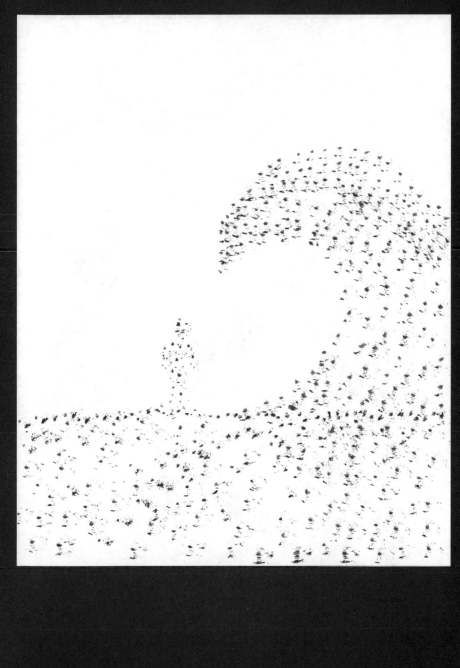

Nothing Rises To Meet Me

I had a thought just then
Nearly did me in
But I hummed and said No
Just to make it go
This is the crude discipline
That keeps me running
A honeycomb spun
Could I spin it any thinner?

Should I hoard all my money
Or spend it all in one night
On the biggest woman
That I can find

Well it doesn't seem to matter much
And worse still this tremendous touch
To conquer what I will
And turn without a chill
And feeling open still
A wanting to be filled

Seek and ye shall find
Ye need more seeking time
And when I overcome
Nothing rises to meet me

Destroy everything
Examine the remains
Destroy everything
Rebuild it's a game

This is the crude discipline
That keeps me running

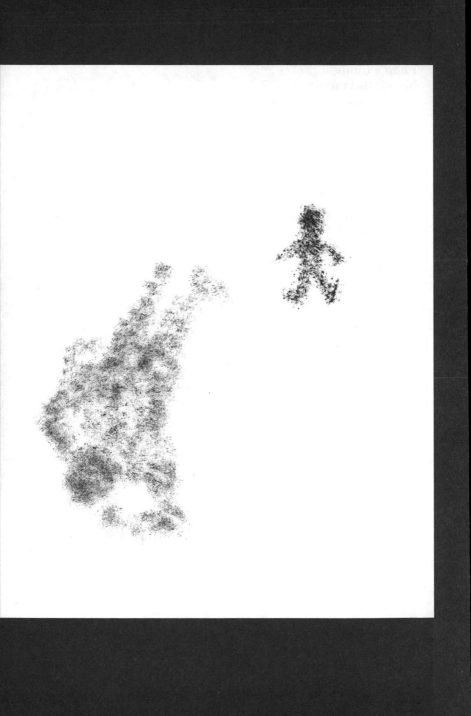

Let me in, I have stigmata too!

One Fine Morning

One fine morning
I'm gonna ride out
Yeah one fine morning
I'm gonna ride right out
Just me and the skeleton crew

We're gonna ride out in a country kind of silence
We're gonna ride out in a country silence
One fine morning

Yeah it's all coming back to me now
My apocalypse!

The curtain rose and burned in the morning sun
Yeah the curtain rose and burned in the morning sun

And the mountains!
And the mountains bowed down
In the morning sun
Like a ballet
Yeah the mountains bowed down
Like a ballet
Of the heart
In the morning sun

And the baby and we all lay in state
Yeah the baby and we all lay in state
And I said Hey! no more drovering!

When the earth turns cold
And the earth turns black
Will I feel you riding on my back?
Yeah when the earth turns cold
And the earth turns black
Will I feel you riding on my back?

For I am a part of the road
Yeah I am a part of the road
The hardest part

My apocalypse
DC 4 5 0
DC 4 5 0

Our Anniversary

It's our anniversary
I leave it ajar
And go outside
To look at the driveway stars

The crickets are chirping
They stop at my step
I stop my step
And they start up again

It's our anniversary and the bullfrogs
And everything that can sing
Is singing its mating song

The soil is steaming
Grass is swooning
Guns or fireworks are popping
Down in the town
A woman is running
A man jumps up and down

It's our anniversary and you've hidden my keys
This is one anniversary you're spending with me

I slide in the front seat
The driver's side
To hotwire and hightail crosses my mind
But still in the driveway
Fixed like stars
I flip on the headlights
And go back inside

Where the climate's controlled
While the battery dies
Clipping the wings
Of your morning flight

The night will end in
Some form of excess
Pants around ankles
Too weak to fully undress

It's our anniversary
A celebration of
And here's to next year
Maybe you'll join me in my car
We'll drive together
But not too far

We are far from flowers
Cut and dried
So let us thrive let us thrive
Let us thrive
Just like the weeds
We curse sometimes

Palimpsest

Winter weather is not my soul
But the biding for spring...

Why's everybody looking at me
Like there's something fundamentally wrong
Like I'm a southern bird
That stayed north too long

Winter exposes the nests
And I'm gone

Permanent Smile

Oh God can you feel the sun in your back
Oh God can you see your shadow inky black
on the sand
Oh God can you hear the saltwater
drying on your skin
Oh God can you feel my heart beating
In my tongue

Oh God by being quiet I hope to alleviate my debt
Oh God by sitting still I hope to lighten your load

And when your shadow covers me from head to toe
And curtonevrae flies tell me it's my time to go
Seven waves of insects make babies in my skin
Seven waves of insects make families in my skin
It's just like animals at play
And the flesh rotted off my skull
And then I will have earned my permanent smile

Oh God I never never ask why

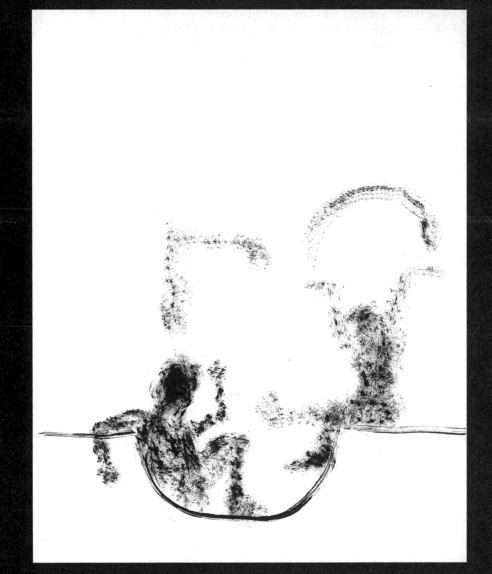

Prince Alone in the Studio

Prince alone in the studio
It's 2 a.m. and all the girls are gone
The girls thought they were going to be able
To have sex with him
They wore their special underwear

Once the tracks were laid down
Prince's back turned around
Raspberry headphones on his head
Are you still here?

Prince alone in the studio
It's 3 a.m.
Prince hasn't eaten in 18 hours
Dinner's burned on the stove
But Prince he doesn't even know

Prince alone in the studio
It's 4 a.m.
And he finally gets that guitar track right
And it's better than anything any girl could ever give him
Because Prince is alone
Prince is alone
Oh Prince you are so alone

And when it's all complete
When it's all complete
He feels like a hunter on the street

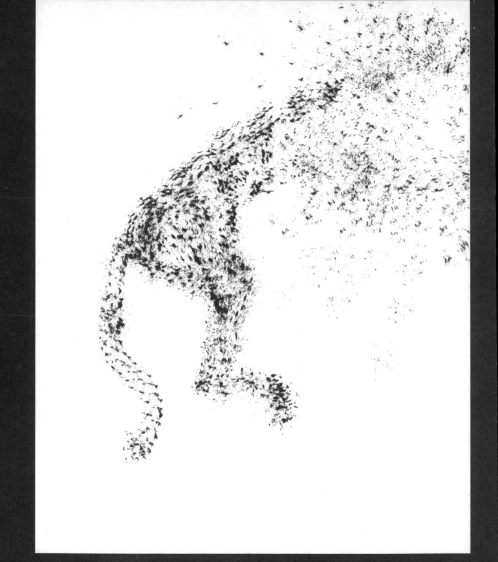

Red Apples

I went down to the river
To meet the widow
She gave me an apple
It was red

I slept in her black arms
For a century
She wanted nothing in return
I gave her nothing in return
I gave her nothing in return

The ghost of her husband
Beautiful as a horse
Pulled up an apple cart
Full of millions of red apples

For us

Ride My Arrow

I don't ever want to die
Do you know this arrow when it arches high
To meet the eagle in the sky?

The eagle flies using the river as a map
A small animal in its clasp
Alive and enjoying the ride

Is life a ride to ride
Or a story to shape and confide
Or chaos neatly denied?

Some people find the taste of pilgrim guts to be too strong
Me I find I can't get by without them for too long
Tear at the flesh tear at the bone
Of anyone who tells you the known is unknown
'Cause life ain't confidential
It's not
It isn't
And it ain't confidential

Ride my arrow

The land I love is splitting in two
Again and again and again
War muddies the river
And getting out we're dirtier than getting in

Ride my arrow

Riding for the Feeling

It's never easy to say goodbye to the faces
So rarely do we see another one so close and
So long

I asked the room if I'd said enough
No one really answered
They just said
Don't go don't go don't go

Well all this leaving is never ending
I kept hoping for one more question or for someone to say
Who do you think you are?
So I could tell them
With intensity
A drop evaporates by law
In conclusion leaving is easy
When you've got some place you need to be
Aw I'm giving up this gig for another season

With the TV on mute
I'm listening back to the tapes
On the hotel bed
My my my apocalypse

I realized I had said very little about waves or wheels
Or riding for the feeling
Riding for the feeling
Is the fastest way to reach the shore on water or land
Riding for the feeling

What if I had stood there at the end
And said again and again and again and again and again
In answer to every question
Riding for the feeling
Riding for the feeling
Riding for the feeling

River Guard

When I take the prisoners swimming
They have the times of their lives

I love to watch them floating
On their backs
Unburdened and relaxed

I sit in the tall grass and look the other way
And when I haul them in they always say
Our sentences will not served

We are constantly on trial
It's a way to be free

Most nights I go for a drive
To the highest place I can find
I'm standing on a cliff with gooseflesh
Watching the wind rip the leaves from the trees

Death defying
Every breath is death defying

Soon we will all be back in the yard
Behind the walls
Living hard
Dreaming of cool rivers and tall grass

We are constantly on trial
It's a way to be free

Rock Bottom Riser

I love my mother
I love my father
I love my sisters too

I bought this guitar
To pledge my love
To pledge my love to you

I am a rock
Bottom riser
And I owe it all to you

I saw a gold ring
At the bottom of the river
Glinting
At my foolish heart
Oh my foolish heart
Had to go diving
Diving diving
Into the murk

And from the bottom of the river
I looked up for the sun
Which had shattered in the water
And the pieces were raining down
Like gold rings
That passed through my hands
As I thrashed and grabbed
I started rising rising

I left my mother
I left my father
Left my sisters too
I left them standing on the banks
And they pulled me out
Of this mighty mighty river

I am a rock
Bottom riser
And I owe it all to you

Say Valley Maker

With the grace of a corpse
In a riptide
I let go
And I slide slide slide
Downriver
With an empty case by my side
An empty case
That's my crime

And I sing (Say Valley Maker)
To keep from cursing
Yes I sing (Say Valley Maker)
To keep from cursing

River Oh
River End
River Oh
River End
River Go
River Bend

Take me through the sweet valley
Where your heart blooms
Take me through the sweet valley
Where your heart is covered in dew

And when the river dries
Will you bury me in wood
Where the river dries
Will you bury me in stone

Oh I never really realized
Death is what it meant
To make it on my own

Because there is no love
Where there is no obstacle
And there is no love
Where there is no bramble
There is no love
On the hacked away plateau
And there is no love
In the unerring
And there is no love
On the one true path

Oh I cantered out here
Now I'm galloping back

So bury me in wood
And I will splinter
Bury me in stone
And I will quake
Bury me in water
And I will geyser
Bury me in fire
And I'm gonna phoenix

I'm gonna phoenix

Seagull

A barroom may entice a seagull like me
Right off the sea
Right off the sea
And into the barroom

And let go yeah let go of the trapeze
And melt the snow of dream river

I wonder if I'll ever wake up
I mean really wake up
Wake up and wake you too
First thing that I will do I will wake you too

How long have I been gone?
How long have I been traveling?
And how tired have I been?
And how far have I got in circling and circling and circling?

With all the tolls we pay
We'll own the highway someday

And the weight of the world slips away

And the seagull falls back on the sea

The Sing

Drinking while sleeping strangers
Unknowingly keep me company
In the hotel bar

Looking out a window that isn't there
Looking at the carpet and the chairs

The only words I've said today are beer and thank you
Beer
Thank you
Beer
Thank you
Beer

Giving praise in a quiet way
Like a church
Like a church
Like a church that's far away

Now I've got limitations like Marvin Gaye
Mortal joy is that way

Outside a train sings its whale song
To a long long train
Long long gone
Then silence comes back alone
High as scaffolding

'Til the wind finds something to ping
Or the pinging things finds the wind

We're all looking for a body
Or a means to make one sing

Small Plane

You used to take me up
I watched and learned how to fly
No navigation system beyond our eyes
Watching

I always went wrong in the same place
Where the river splits towards the sea
That couldn't possibly be
You and me

Sometimes you sleep while I take us home
That's when I know we really have a home

I never like to land
Getting back up seems impossibly grand
We do it with ease

Danger I never think of danger
I really am a lucky man
I really am a lucky man flying this small plane

I like it when I take the controls from you
And when you
take the controls from me

I really am a lucky man
I really am a lucky man flying this small plane

Eyes scan the path
Ahead and all around

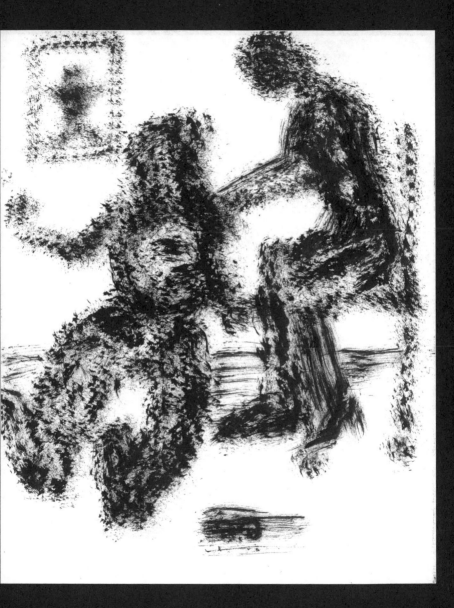

Spring

The wind is pushing the clouds along
Out of sight
A power is putting them away
A power that moves things erotically
Like a widow with a rosary

Everything is awing and tired of praise
Mountains don't need my accolades
And spring looks bad lately anyway
Like death warmed over

And the bantam is preening madly
Waiting for the light of day

And all I want to do is to make love to you
With a careless mind
Who cares what's mine?
With a careless careless careless mind

We call it spring though things are dying
Connected to the land like a severed hand
And I see our house on a hill on a clear blue morning
When I am out walking
My eyes are still forming
The door I walk through and I see
The true spring is in you
The true spring is in you

My wide worlds collide
And mind wide words collide
And seasons kaleidoscoping

And all I want to do is to make love to you
In the fertile dirt in the fertile dirt
With a careless mind
With a careless careless careless mind

Strayed

It's strange the way
You walk behind
But seem to lead the way

I know I have strayed

I have taken you for a ride
Left you waiting in the car
While I played death games inside

I know I have strayed

I have loved in haste
I've been an alleycat and a bumblebee
To your panther and your wasp
Oh I have loved
While thinking only of the cost

I know I have strayed

I've raised a sick child to your lips
And in asking you to kiss
What I would not kiss

I know I have strayed

Well I never thought I'd be
One of those men
With pin-ups on their wall
For all to see
I thought that was just mechanics

I know I have strayed

I have taken you for a ride
Left you waiting in the car
While I played death games inside

Summer Painter

I painted names on boats for a summer
For luck you keep the same first letter
You don't want bad luck at sea

Rich Man's Folly and Poor Man's Dream
I painted these while beavers built dams all around me

Come September come Fall
Holding a job was not believable behavior at all
So I split
But like a beaver is a dam builder
You never really quit
I made some dough and I socked it away
I always said for a rainy day
I never truly knew who I was working for anyway
The rich or the poor
Who am I working for
The rich or the poor?

When the hurricane hit
Some found it suspicious that I'd just since left the frame
Like all that time spent down by the water
Had somehow given me control over the rain
And some people say wrongly that I wash things away
Guess I got my rainy day

Like a sorcerer's cape!
The rain ripped the lips
Off the mouth of the bay
And rendered the eye
And sleighted the hand
And tricked the land
And blew the air away

Then came a quiet
No one should know

Rich Man's Folly and Poor Man's Dream
I'm painting these while beavers build dams all around me

Like this?

Teenage Spaceship

Flying around
The houses at night
Flying alone

A teenage spaceship
I was a teenage spaceship

Landing at night
I was beautiful with all my lights

Loomed so large on the horizon
So large
People thought my windows
Were stars
So large on the horizon
People thought my windows
Were stars

A teenage spaceship

And I swore I'd never lay like a log
Or bark like a dog

I was a teenage smog
Sewn to the sky

37 Push Ups

47 push ups
in a winter rates
seaside motel

I feel like Travis Bickle
I'm listening to Highway to Hell
It's a shitty little tape I taped off the radio

39 push ups
in a winter rates
seaside motel

32 push ups
in a winter rates
seaside motel

Not looking too good
Not feeling so well

37 push ups
in a winter rates seaside motel

I'm going up again
Going up to go down again

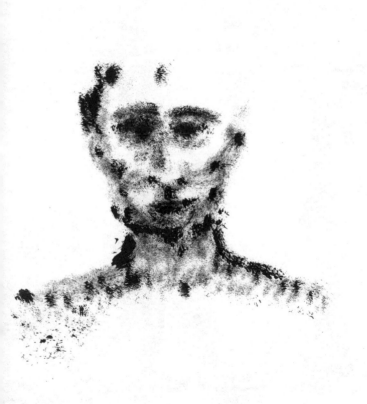

To Be of Use

Most of my fantasies are of
Making someone else come
Most of my fantasies are of
To be of use
To be of some hard
Simple
Undeniable use

Like a spindle
Like a candle
Like a horseshoe
Like a corkscrew

To be of use
To be of use

Most of my fantasies are of
Making someone else come
On a horse
Over palms laid
On the threshold
Of the coming day

Coming day
Coming day
Come

Truth Serum

Me and some friends of mine
We stayed up all night taking truth serum
We soon realized the mistake we made
And went our separate separate ways

I went up on the roof
Where I thought I'd find some truth
There beneath the stairs
But questions followed me

Do you miss me when I go?
Honey I love you and that's all you need to know
Well then what is love?
Love is an object kept in an empty box
How can something be in an empty box?
Well well give me another shot
Of that truth serum

I went back downstairs to check on my friends
Because truth has a way of beginning an end
Big Bruiser Ken walks in says
I like men
I excuse myself and go back on the roof again

More questions followed me
Is death really the end?
Honey I love you and that's all you need to know
Well then what is life?
Well that's a good song
(sings) Without you by my side

People people there's a lesson here plain to see
There's no truth in you
There's no truth in me
The truth is between
The truth is between

The Wind and the Dove

Somewhere between the wind and the dove
Lies all I sought in you
And when the wind just dies
And the dove won't rise
From your window sill

Well I cannot tell you
Which way it would be
If it was not this way too
For the wind and the dove

And I am a child of linger on
I peer through the window gone

Somewhere between the wind and the dove
Lies all I lost in you
And when the wind just dies
And the dove won't rise
From your window sill

Well I cannot tell you
Which way it would be
If it was not this way too
For the wind and the dove

And I am a child of linger on
I peer through the window gone

Too Many Birds

Too many birds in one tree
And the sky is full of black and screaming leaves
The sky is full of black and screaming

And one more bird
Then one more bird
And one last bird
And another

One last black bird without a place to land
One last black bird without a place to be
Turns around in hopes to find the place it last knew rest
Oh black bird over black grain burned
This is not where you last knew rest
You fly all night to sleep on stone
The heartless rest that in the morn will be gone
You fly all night to sleep on stone to return to the tree
With too many birds

If
If you
If you could
If you could only
If you could only stop
If you could only stop your
If you could only stop your heart
If you could only stop your heart beat
If you could only stop your heart beat for
If you could only stop your heart beat for one heart
If you could only stop your heart beat for one heart beat

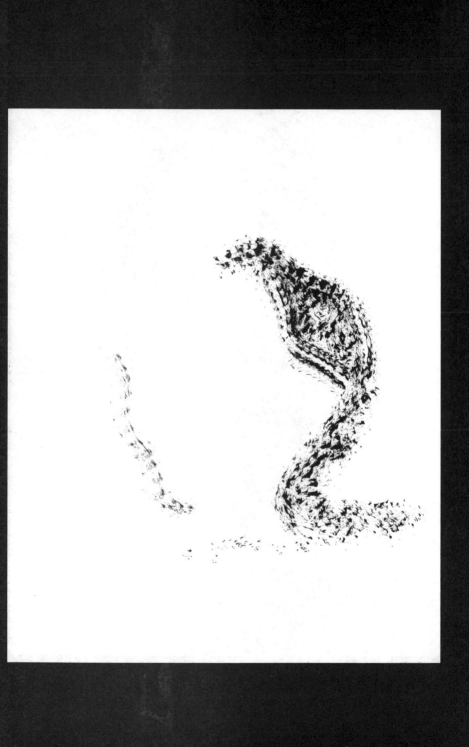

Rococo Zephyr

She lay beside me like a branch from a tender willow tree
I was as still as still as a river could be
When a rococo zephyr swept over her and me
She watched the water ripple ripple ripple ripple light
Light watched the water ripple ripple ripple ripple her
She did some kind of dance
Jaunty as a bee
I tried to look my best
A finch in wild mint vest

A fiercer force had wrenched her from where she used to be
I caught and caressed the length of her
A tender willow branch floating on me
Well maybe this was all was all that's meant to be
Maybe this is all is all that's meant to be
A rococo zephyr crept up and stepped over her and me

Well I used to be sort of blind
Now I can sort of see

Sycamore

There's sap in the trees if you tap 'em
There's blood on the seas if you map 'em
Christiaan if you see your papa tell him I love him
He taught me to love in the wild and fight in the gym
He taught me the bottle gives birth to the cup
And you won't get hurt if you just keep your hands up
And stand tall like sycamore

Sycamore got to grow down to grow up
Young roots grip the soil like baby's first cup
And when they bend you in two
And say too green for the fire
When all you want to do is be a part of the fire
All you want to do is be the fire part of fire
Like sycamore

There's sap in the trees if you tap 'em
There's blood on the seas if you map 'em
Christiaan when I see your papa I'll tell him you love him
And remember to love in the wild and fight in the gym
Remember the bottle gives birth to the cup
And you won't get hurt if you just keep your hands up
And stand tall like sycamore

Universal Applicant

Without work's calving increments
Or love's coltish punch
What would I be?
An animaless isthmus
Beyond the sea

Oh bees only swarm when they're looking for a home
So I followed them
I found the bees nest in the buffalo's chest
I drank their honey that milk
I've seen this taste cased in almost every face
That's working to see it in all
And this kidnaps me

Tied up in a boat and kicked off to sea
In tight baby binding technique
My arm chews through the swaddling slings
There's a flare gun in my hand
I point it straight and point it high
And to the universe it applies

It lit things up in lavender
Where I'd been
Was
Might go
I saw the calf
I saw the bees
I saw the bison oh!
And the colt
Well I'm sure they all laughed at me
At me solo in my boat

The flare burned and fell
The boat burned as well

And the punk
And the lunk
And the drunk
And the skunk
And the hunk
And the monk
All sunk

Vessel in Vain

I can't be held responsible for the things I say
For I am just a vessel in vain
And I can't be held responsible for the things I see
For I am just a vessel in vain

No boat out on no ocean
No name there on no hull
And it's not a strain at all to remember
Those that I've left behind
They're all standing right here beside me now
And most of them with a smile

My ideals have got me on the run
Towards my connection with everyone
My ideals have got me on the run
That's my connection with everyone

Such free reign
For a vessel in vain

The Well

I could not work
So I threw a bottle into the woods
And then I felt bad
For the doe paw
And the rabbit paw
So I went looking for the pieces
Of the bottle that I threw
Because I could not work

I went deep
Further than I could throw
And I came upon an old abandoned well
All boarded over
With a drip hanging from the bucket still

Well I watched that drip but it would not drop
I watched that drip but it would not drop
I knew what I had to do
Had to pull those boards off the well

When I got the boards off
I stared into the black black black
And you know I had to yell
Just to get my voice back

I guess everybody has their own thing
That they yell into a well

I gave it a couple hoots
A hello
And a fuck all y'all

I guess everybody has their own thing
That they yell into a well

And as I stood like that
Staring into the black black black
I felt a cool wet kiss
On the back of my neck

Dang

I knew if I stood up
The drip would roll down my back
Into no man's land

So I stayed like that
Staring into the black black black

Well they say black is all colors at once
So I gave it my red rage my yellow streak
The greenest parts of me
And my blues
I knew just what I had to do

I had to turn around and go back
And let that drip roll down my back
And I felt so bad about that

But wouldn't you know
When I turned to go
Another drip was forming
On the bottom of the bucket
And I felt so good about that

The Wheel

The wheel has turned one full circle
Time for my meal of wood
To make my home Lord
In a stable spoke Lord
Inside a turning wheel would be good
To make my home Lord
In a stable spoke Lord
Inside a turning wheel bound for good

A wood bee tries to find purchase
On a turning spoke
From Memphis to Potomac
Never giving up hope

I'd die in your jails Lord
But you'd die by my laws Lord
I think you got it worse

No rebel I Lord
I follow the river
When I'm lost

The wheel has turned one more circle
The payload is now immense
So climb aboard all climb aboard
Because the heavier we get
The harder we crush

The wagon rolls like an old millstone
Driving bad deeds six feet deep

To make my home Lord
In a stable spoke Lord
Inside a turning wheel
Would be good

To make my home Lord
In a stable spoke Lord
Inside a turning wheel
Bound for good

Winter Road

The road is dangerous
Pretty and white
Tires spinning on snow
World spinning heavy and slow
And I'm headed home

Time itself means nothing
But time spent with you

A Donald Sutherland interview comes on the truck radio
He apologizes to all he's loved and sired

Long shot of my face

I have learned when things are beautiful
To just keep on
Just keep on
When things are beautiful
Just keep on

The blinding lights of the kingdom can make you weep

I have learned when things are beautiful
To just keep on
Just keep on

Daddy's home!